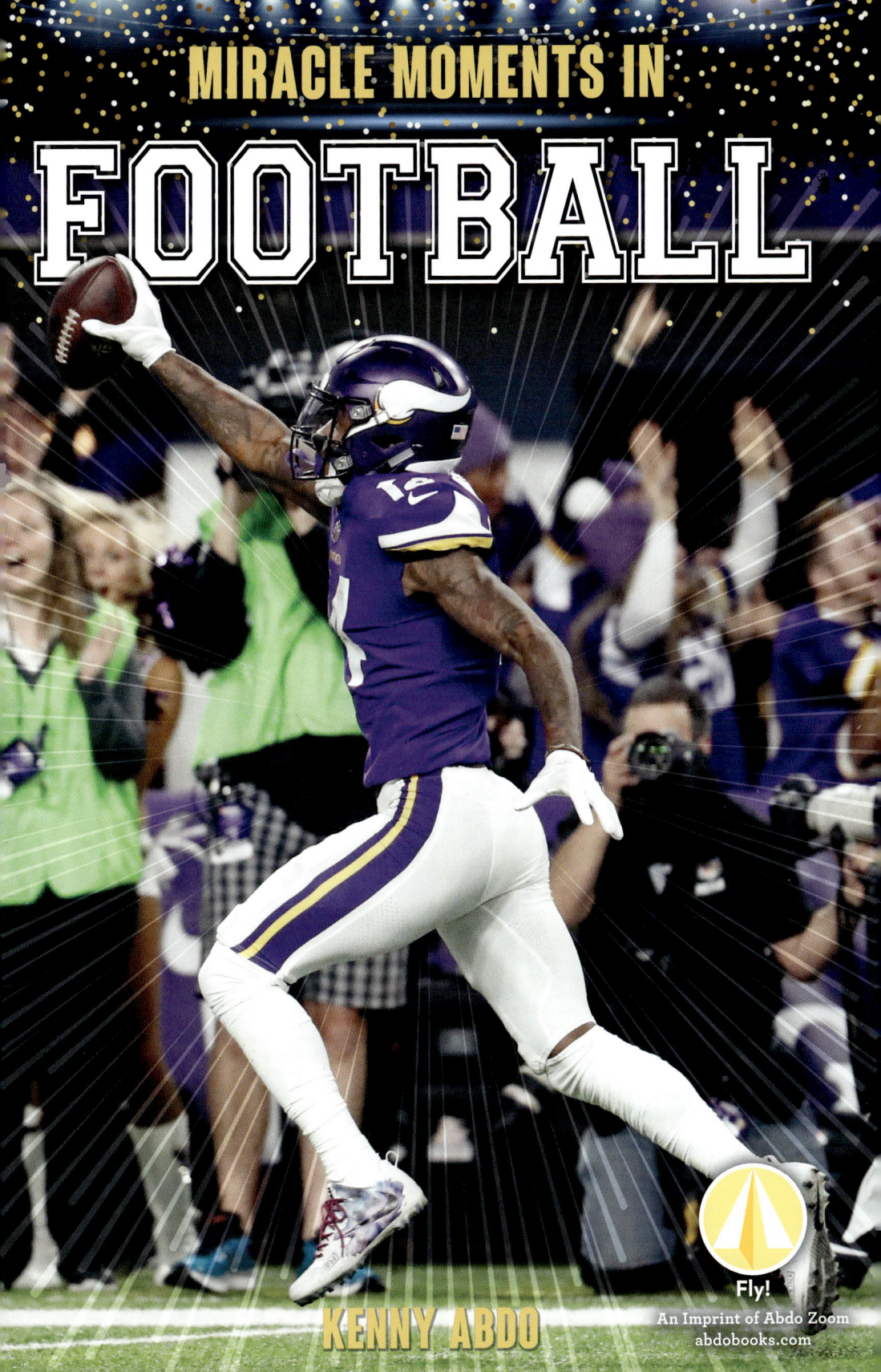

MIRACLE MOMENTS IN
FOOTBALL

KENNY ABDO

Fly!
An Imprint of Abdo Zoom
abdobooks.com

abdobooks.com

Published by Abdo Zoom, a division of ABDO, P.O. Box 398166, Minneapolis, Minnesota 55439. Copyright © 2022 by Abdo Consulting Group, Inc. International copyrights reserved in all countries. No part of this book may be reproduced in any form without written permission from the publisher. Fly!™ is a trademark and logo of Abdo Zoom.

Printed in the United States of America, North Mankato, Minnesota.
052021
092021

THIS BOOK CONTAINS RECYCLED MATERIALS

Photo Credits: Alamy, AP Images, Icon Sportswire, iStock, Newscom, North Wind Picture Archives, Shutterstock
Production Contributors: Kenny Abdo, Jennie Forsberg, Grace Hansen
Design Contributors: Dorothy Toth, Neil Klinepier

Library of Congress Control Number: 2020919507

Publisher's Cataloging-in-Publication Data

Names: Abdo, Kenny, author.
Title: Miracle moments in football / by Kenny Abdo.
Description: Minneapolis, Minnesota : Abdo Zoom, 2022 | Series: Miracles in sports | Includes online resources and index.
Identifiers: ISBN 9781098223205 (lib. bdg.) | ISBN 9781098223908 (ebook) | ISBN 9781098224257 (Read-to-Me ebook)
Subjects: LCSH: Football--History--Juvenile literature. | Football--Records--Juvenile literature. | Sports--History--Juvenile literature. | Miracles--Juvenile literature. | Curiosities and wonders--Juvenile literature.
Classification: DDC 796.332--dc23

TABLE OF CONENTS

Football 4

Do You Believe? 10

Legacy 20

Glossary 22

Online Resources 23

Index 24

FOOTBALL

Going long for more than 100 years, football is a sport hardcore fans cheer for!

The National Football **League** (NFL) was formed in 1920. It was just 10 teams from four states that created the American Professional Football Association (APFA). It was renamed the NFL in 1922.

Since the beginning of pro football, fans have witnessed several miracles on the gridiron, sometimes with the help of a Hail Mary.

DO YOU BELIEVE?

The Eagles trailed the Giants by five points in a 1978 game. A fumble was recovered by Herman Edwards. He ran the ball 26 yards for a winning touchdown! It was named the Miracle at Meadowlands.

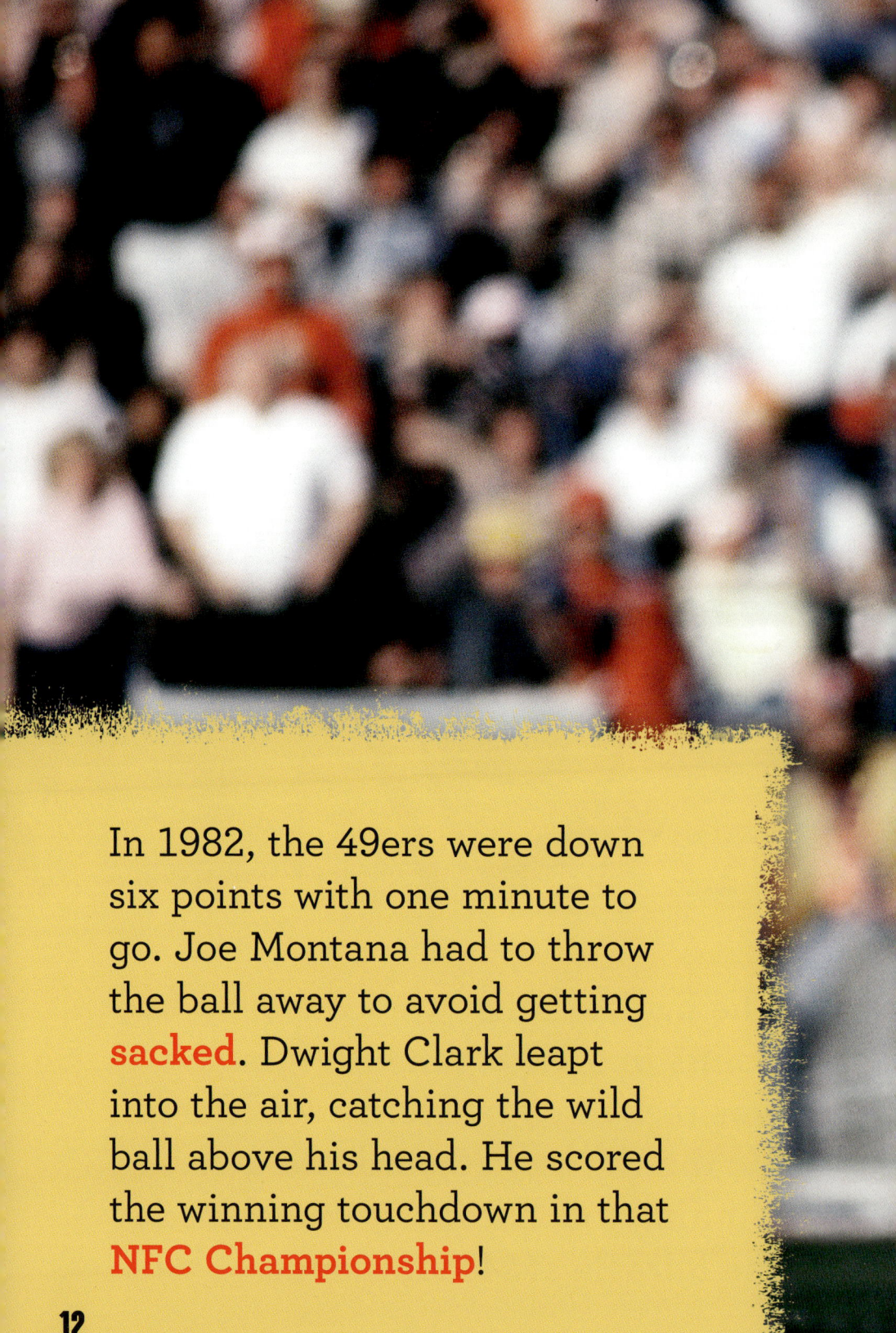

In 1982, the 49ers were down six points with one minute to go. Joe Montana had to throw the ball away to avoid getting **sacked**. Dwight Clark leapt into the air, catching the wild ball above his head. He scored the winning touchdown in that **NFC Championship**!

On January 3, 1993, the Bills were down 35–3 in the third quarter against the Oilers.

The Bills scored an unbelievable 35 **unanswered** points in the fourth quarter. They won the game! It was the largest comeback in NFL history.

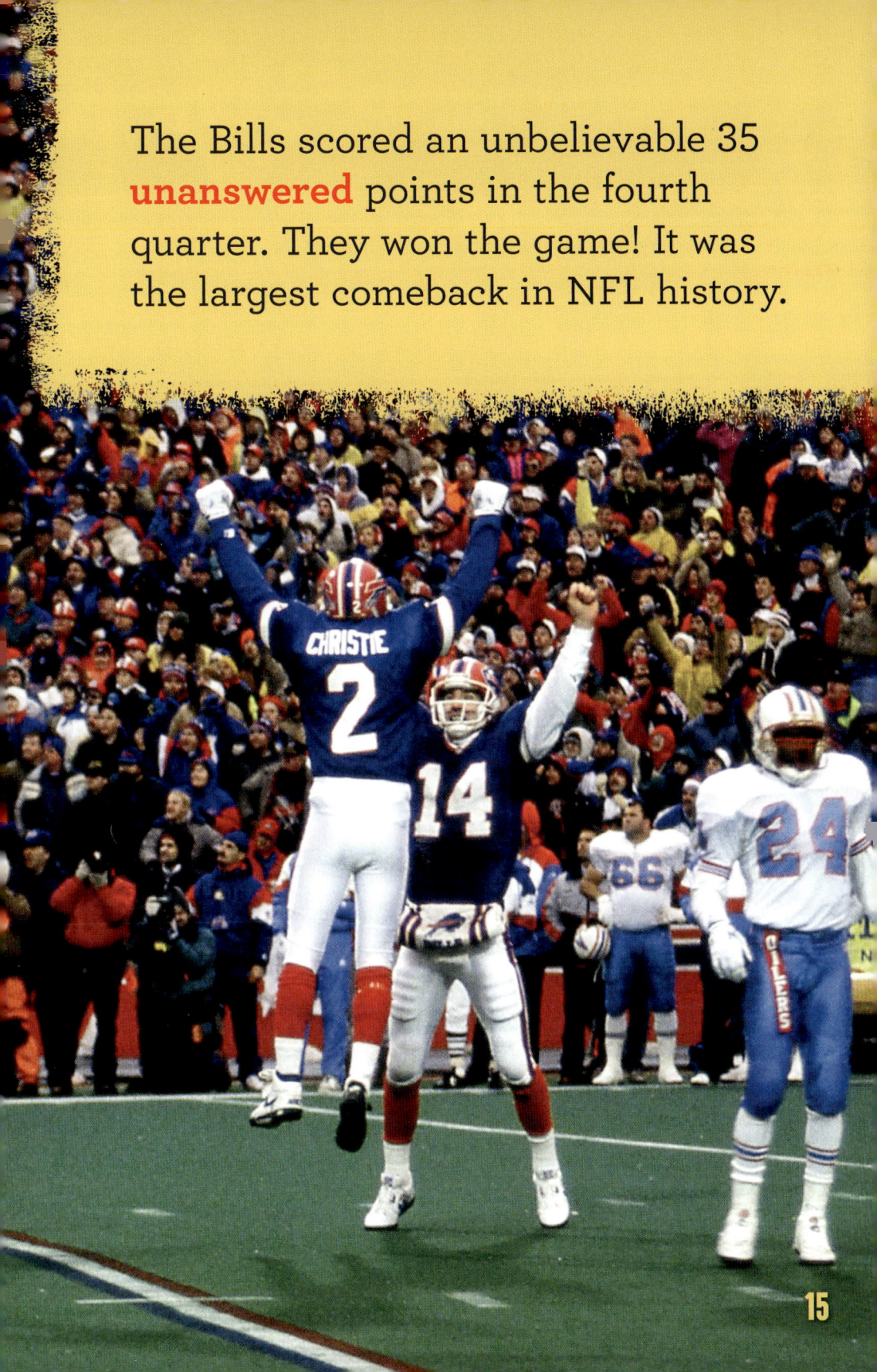

With 10 seconds left in the 2018 divisional playoff game, Stefon Diggs caught a pass from **QB** Case Keenum, and ran 61-yards for a touchdown. The Vikings beat the Saints 29-24 with the play known as the Minneapolis Miracle.

Trailing by 5 points with 7 seconds to go on December 9, 2018, the Dolphins completed two **lateral passes** leaving **running back** Kenyan Drake with the ball. Drake ran 52 yards to solidify the Miami Miracle!

LEGACY

Football's greatest miracles have made it on **highlight reels**, showcasing the greatness every team can achieve.

Whether it is catching the uncatchable or running impossible distances, football inspires every generation to go for the extra point!

GLOSSARY

highlight reel – the best moments of a certain game or athlete compiled into one film.

lateral pass – when the ball carrier passes to a teammate behind him.

league – a group of teams that compete against each other.

NFC Championship – the annual championship of the National Football Conference.

quarterback (QB) – the player on the offensive team that directs teammates in their play.

running back – an offensive player who specifically carries the ball.

sacked – when a quarterback is tackled behind the line of scrimmage while still in possession of the ball.

unanswered – when one team scores many points without the other team scoring.

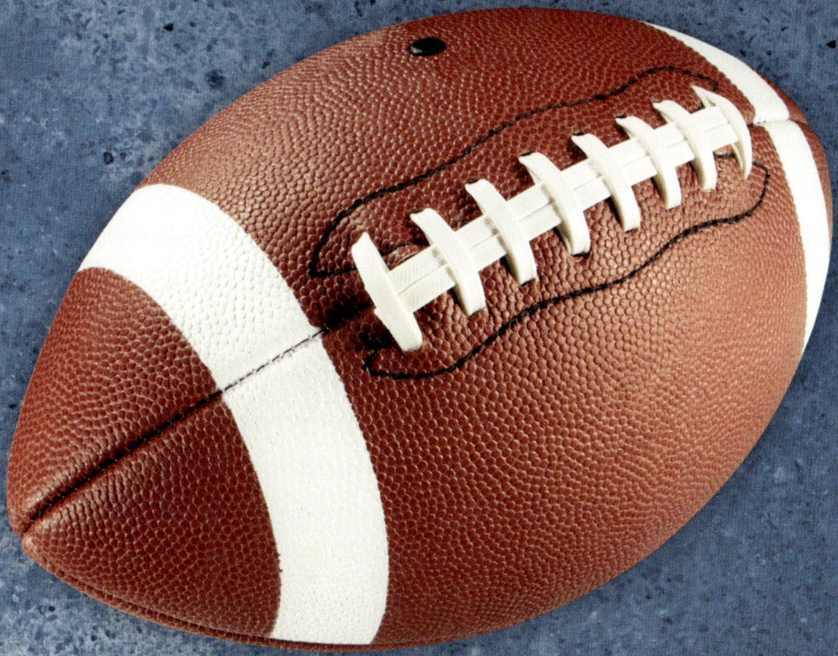

ONLINE RESOURCES

To learn more about miracle moments in football, please visit abdobooklinks.com or scan this QR code. These links are routinely monitored and updated to provide the most current information available.

INDEX

Bills (team) 14, 15

Clark, Dwight 12

Diggs, Stefon 17

Dolphins (team) 19

Drake, Kenyan 19

Eagles (team) 11

Edwards, Herman 11

Giants (team) 11

Keenum, Case 17

Montana, Joe 12

NFC Championship 12

Oilers (team) 14, 15

playoffs 17

Saints (team) 17

Vikings (team) 17